Mommy & Me
A Micro Preemie

By Tameka Tate

Copyright © 2023

Bird House Publishing

8325 Broadway Street, Pearland, TX 77581

(832) 535-2362

Bird House Publishing is committed to filling the need for more diverse books. We are also committed to the relentless pursuit of equity, authenticity, and inclusion. We encourage all of our readers and authors to show up in the world as their best selves. Our stories build empathy, coping skills, courage, and curiosity to explore cultures other than our own. We are always looking for diverse and thoughtful voices to share with the world.

All rights reserved. No part of this book may be reproduced, stored, or transmitted by any means – whether auditory, graphic, mechanical, or electronic – without written permission of the author, except in the case of brief excerpts used in critical articles and reviews. Unauthorized reproduction of any part of this work is illegal and punishable by law.

ISBN: 979-8-9855113-7-6

Because of the dynamic nature of the internet, any web addresses or links contained in this book may have changed since publication and may no longer be valid. The views expressed in this work are solely those of the author and do not necessarily reflect the views of the publisher, and the publisher hereby disclaims any responsibility for them.

Bird House Publishing rev date 2/15/23

Dedication

This book is dedicated to everyone that supported Asher as he fought his way through the NICU! There aren't enough words to convey the appreciation I have for each and every one of you! Thank you so much from Tiny HERO and me!

Asher's Journey Here
Preface:

So, Mommy and Me share the same birthday month. However, I originally was supposed to share the same birthday month as my maternal great-grandmother and pawpaw, but God had other plans. I came super-duper early. I'm talking "no skin and eyes sealed at 23 weeks" early!

The one good thing about that is now I get to share my birthday month with my Mommy in July, the best month in the world! Yes, I'm a summer baby!

Hi! My name is Asher! Some people think my incredible journey started in July 2020, but it actually started before then.

In December 2017, my big sister, Ayrii, was born when Mommy was only 20 weeks pregnant.

Unfortunately, my big sister only lived for 2 hours and 12 minutes, but Mommy got to hold her the entire time, watching her heartbeat.

Mommy was so sad. After losing Ayrii, the idea of having a baby slowly faded away.

Until God and a red bird showed up. That's when God told Mommy to trust Him and give it one more shot. Mommy says the red bird was Ayrii, and she would appear whenever mommy felt sad.

It was an ordinary day in Mommy's belly, or the baby belly factory as I like to call it. I was floating around, relaxing in my amniotic sac. You know, doing the things little growing babies do.

Then out of nowhere, I heard Mommy crying!

I wonder what is happening!

Why is Mommy crying?

Why is everything shaking so fast?

Why is Mommy screaming?

Before I knew it, I was flipped upside down and about to slide down the canal.

But wait! It's not time!

I'm not done preparing for Mommy! My eyes are still sealed; she won't be able to see them!

My little lungs aren't big enough.

I'm too small for the big world. I'm not ready yet!

Please, no! This can't be happening to Mommy again. What can I do? How can I stop myself from sliding?

Mommy can't lose me. She has already lost my sister!

I have to think of a plan before the doctors come for me!

Think, Asher. Think!

I got it! I have to fight like Mommy talked about when she reads to me.

Uh, oh! I'm sliding faster!

Whoooooooooaaaa! Here we go!

Wow, it feels really funny outside of my sac!
And it's really loud out here!

Wait! What are they doing? Why are they putting that down my throat? Where is my Mommy? I can't feel her! I want my Mommy! Please!

Can anyone hear me?

Please! Mommy needs to know I'm okay. Does she know? Please, somebody, tell Mommy I'm going to fight! I promise!

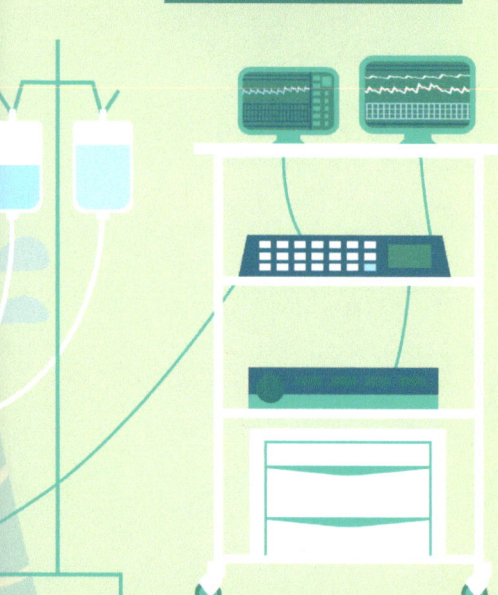

Because Asher was so tiny, the doctors had to intubate him by putting something like a straw down his throat to help him breathe because his lungs were not big enough yet, and he was placed in what is called an incubator.

While Asher was thinking of a plan, little did he know that he was about to take his first helicopter ride. Because Asher needed extra and special care, he was transferred to Children's Memorial Hermann Hospital, the biggest medical center in the country. Unfortunately, his little eyes were still sealed, so he didn't see the view from above, but the doctors were sure to let Mommy know he was going for a ride. But before he flew across the city, he got to see Mommy.

Hey, I'm moving! Where are they taking me? Wait a minute, is that… is that Mommy? Yes, that's her! I hear her voice. Mommy, I'm here! I'm okay. Are you okay? They have this weird thing down my throat so I can breathe, I think, and it feels weird not lying next to your heartbeat…

How will I rest without you? I'm so scared!
Can you hold me?

Asher was so sad because he wanted to be in Mommy's arms, but he was just too small, and it would take a while before Mommy got to hold him. After a short visit with Mommy, the emergency team had to hurry and fly Asher across town to the newborn intensive care unit, or NICU, where he would get around-the-clock care. Once he arrived, doctors ran many tests to see exactly what he needed to be comfortable for his new adventure.

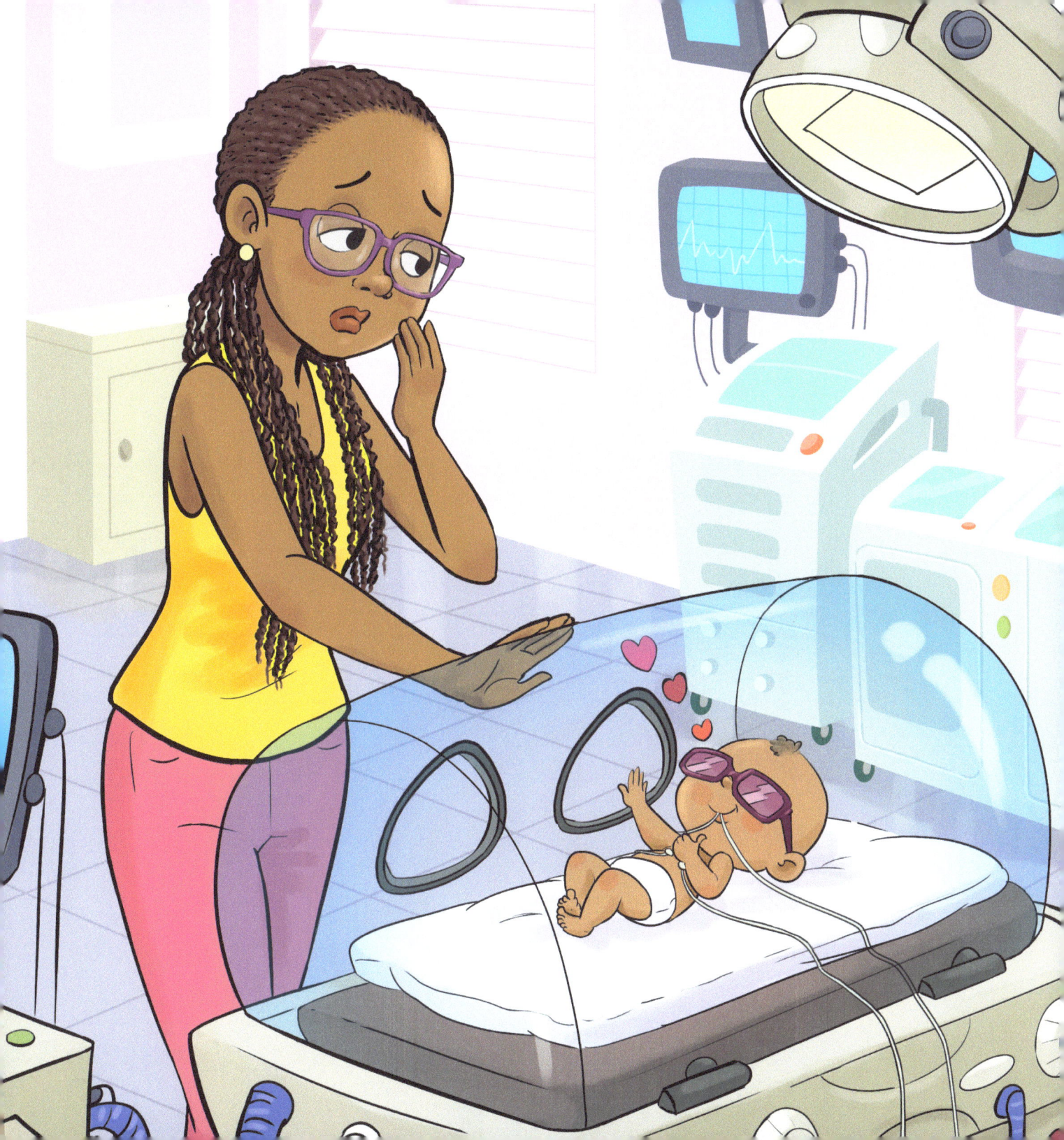

I made it! I'm at the Children's Memorial Hermann Hospital, 7th floor.

It's so cold in here!

I wonder why the top of my incubator is off. Incubator. That's such a funny word!

I'm going to call my incubator my submarine tank. That sounds way cooler!

The "Submarine Tank" is clear, with two round doors on each side so the doctors and nurses can put their hands in to take care of Asher. The top also comes off when Asher needs a wipe-down or for emergencies.

The nurses came to take care of me. She held my hand and told me not to be scared.

My eyes were still sealed, so I couldn't see anything around me, but I could hear all the doctors and nurses when they came around my tank.

When they left, I yawned. I'm sleepy.

The following morning, while Asher was still sleeping, he had scans on his brain to see if there was any bleeding. Later that evening, after his long nap, Asher felt a warm sensation all over his body. It was very familiar, but he didn't quite know what it was. The feeling scared Asher so bad his heart rate started to increase.

My heart is pumping so fast! I don't know what is going on!

Asher's heart monitor started to beep, alerting the nurse to check on him. But before the nurse got to him, Asher realized something.

Wait a minute! I know that voice! I think that's my… MOMMY!

It's Mommy! It's Mommy! She's finally here. I missed her so much!

Mommy was finally released from the hospital and came straight to see Asher. She could not live another day without being by Asher's bedside. Asher's heart rate increased as Mommy got closer to his POD. But, the moment Mommy got to him, his heart rate went down, and the alarms on his monitor stopped beeping.

The doctors met with her, explaining everything going on with Asher. Asher was really sick because he was so small. His left lung had collapsed, and he had jaundice which required him to be placed under a blue light. An ultrasound of his head revealed a Grade 2 brain bleed on the left and a Grade 4 on the right, which was the most severe. He also needed blood and platelets. The doctors and nurses gave him the attention he needed, and he slept a lot for the first few weeks. But then Asher got really sick!

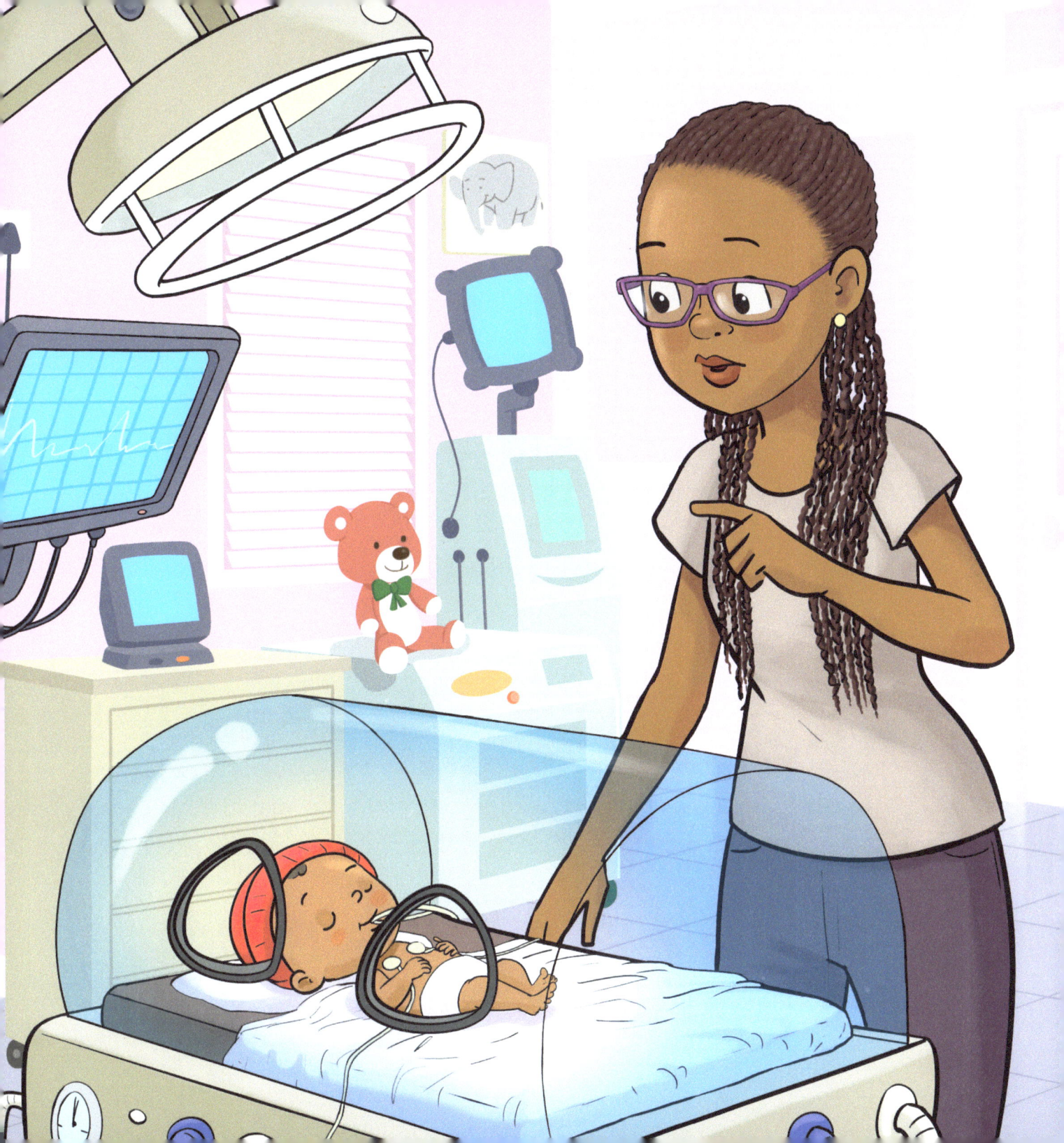

Beep! Beep! Beep! Beep! Beep!

What's that sound? I hear someone saying "Code Blue! Code Blue!" and they sound really loud!

At about 4 am, mommy received a call in her room saying they needed her to come to Asher's bedside. He was coding, meaning his heart and breathing were in trouble. They had to start CPR, a life-saving technique. Asher's little lungs weren't doing well.

Mommy's heart was pounding so hard. She could hear it in her ears!

All the lights were on in the pod as the doctors worked on Asher.

Mommy was frozen as she stood by the door, holding her breath, wishing she could give her last one to him.

The sound of the air blasting inside Asher's lungs as they compressed the bag over and over was like a giant wave crashing on the shore, except this sound wasn't relaxing. Instead, it only made Mommy's heart pound harder and harder.

Alarms were ringing loud, and the ventilator lights were blinking.

Everything was moving so fast, but to Mommy, things were going in slow motion.

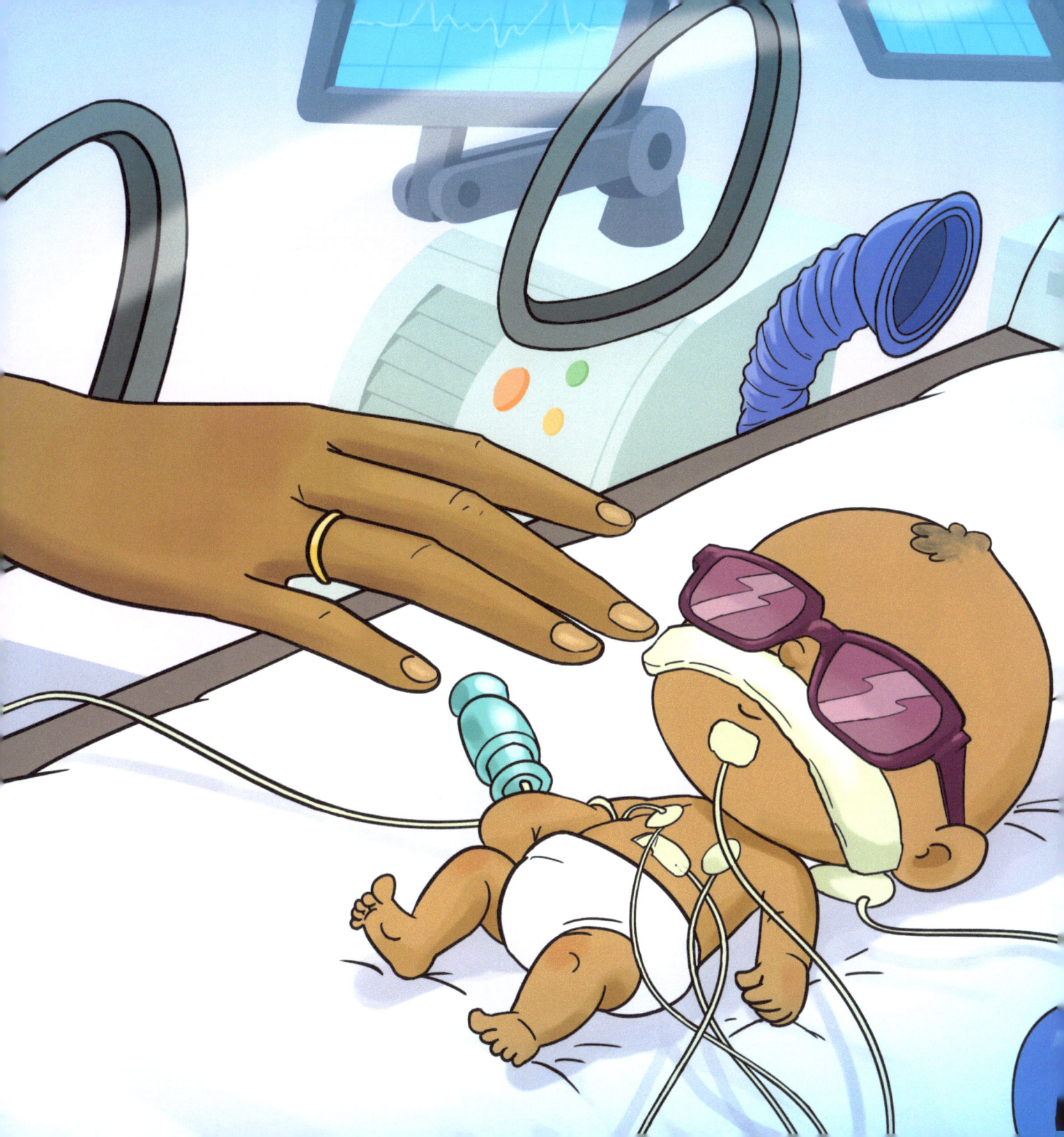

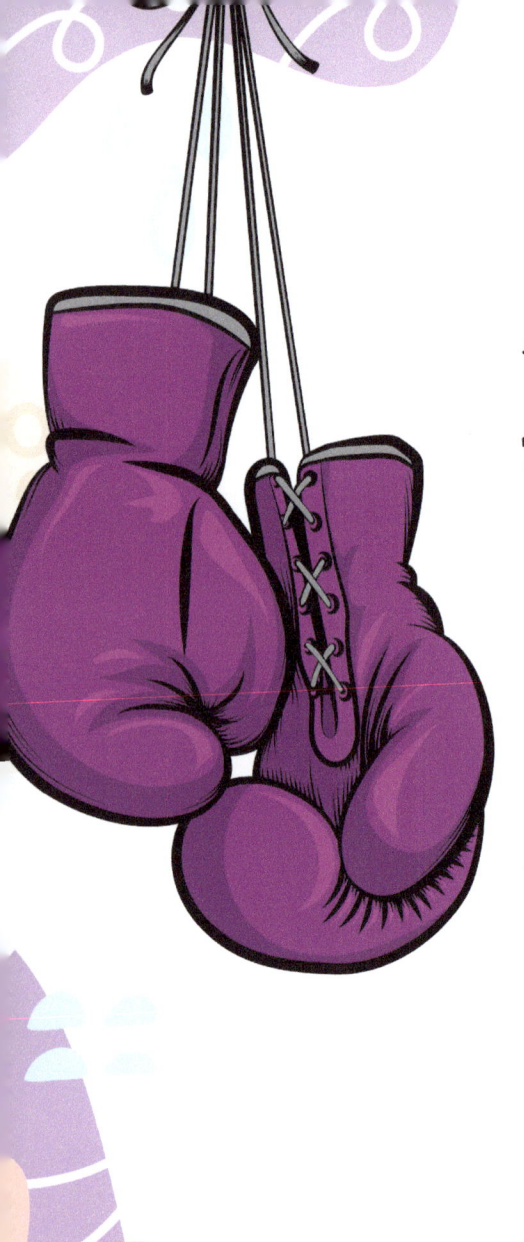

After about five minutes, which felt like hours to Mommy, the alarms stopped.
The compressions stopped. The doctors looked at one another with a sigh of relief. He was back! He was breathing!

Mommy fell to her knees with tears in her eyes, thanking God for keeping Asher alive! Little did she know Asher was fighting hard just as he promised, especially because it was Mommy's birthday.

Mommy walked up to Asher's tank with tears falling down her face. She was shaking and terrified. His little skin was purple and blue.

Asher was so sad for scaring mommy and making her cry. All he wanted to do was to make her feel better. Then, weakly, Asher began to think to himself.

Mommy, I know you can't hear me, but I'm okay.
I just needed some help breathing. The air pockets got into my lungs, and I needed some help.

I'm so sorry for scaring you like that on your birthday. Please, forgive me!

Mommy reached for Asher's little hand while staring at him, and suddenly, his tiny little eyes opened.

Happy Birthday, Mommy! I love you so much!

Mommy was ecstatic. She began shouting to the nurses, telling them to come and see. The birthday that started as a nightmare turned into a beautiful surprise!

Poop, Asher. Poop!

Gosh, my tummy is hurting.

I wonder if it's from the new medicine
they gave for my low blood pressure.

Hmm...

I don't remember them telling Mommy
it would make my tummy hurt.

I know I need to poop, but I can't. I've been
trying for days, and it's too hard!

Asher's blood pressure has been low for a few weeks.
Therefore, he had to start a medication named dopamine.
After a few days, Mommy got concerned with the color of
his belly and how big it had gotten. Finally, Mommy told the nurse she
wanted the doctor to look into it. After a few exams, it was determined
that Asher needed surgery to remove a small portion of his bowel; and an
ostomy bag placed on his belly for 6 to 8 weeks. This bag would collect his
bowels until his body could remove the waste on its own.

Poop, Asher. Poop!

Gosh, my tummy is hurting.

I wonder if it's from the new medicine
they gave for my low blood pressure.

Hmm…

I don't remember them telling Mommy
it would make my tummy hurt.

I know I need to poop, but I can't. I've been
trying for days, and it's too hard!

Asher's blood pressure has been low for a few weeks.
Therefore, he had to start a medication named dopamine.
After a few days, Mommy got concerned with the color of
his belly and how big it had gotten. Finally, Mommy told the nurse she
wanted the doctor to look into it. After a few exams, it was determined
that Asher needed surgery to remove a small portion of his bowel; and an
ostomy bag placed on his belly for 6 to 8 weeks. This bag would collect his
bowels until his body could remove the waste on its own.

Whenever Mommy gets nervous
or sad or even happy, she writes poems.

The Anxiety of a Mother
One thought after another
the anxieties of being a mother.

Trapped in the pits of my anatomy,
How? How can this be?

I haven't held my baby.
Forty-eight days of misery.
But I'm looking at you blissfully.

I wonder what your skin feels like,
up against mine, squeezing you tight.
I dream of it every night,
holding you close, snuggled up just right.

Reading you stories, singing you songs,
watching you grow and carry on.

My little baby, the love of my life,
keep pushing. Keep putting up a fight.
Mommy is here, right by your side, every day
and every night.

My Baby Boy
A poem from Mommy

A tiny little human once lived in me during my ultrasound days.
I couldn't wait to see.
Ten little fingers. Ten little toes.
Two little eyes. One little nose
11/7 was the day we were supposed to meet,
but on 7/11, you came to me.
Twenty-three weeks and zero days,
now in the NICU, where you will spend your first days.
Brain bleeds, air in your lungs,
low blood pressure, and our journey has just begun!

My anxiety and nerves get the best of me,
but I know I have to depend on my G-O-D!
My Asher! My son, please fight for me.
I promise I'll be the best Mommy I could be!

Today is the best day! From my submarine tank, I saw Mommy! She came in, and the nurse gave her a gown. Mommy sat in the recliner in my room. Then the nurse picked me up from my submarine tank and placed me right on Mommy's chest!

Mommy's heart was beating so fast, and a big Kool-Aid smile was plastered on her face!

The nurse said, "Okay, mom, you have one hour of skin-to-skin because we don't want him to be out for too long."

"One hour is good for me," Mommy said with excitement.

I finally got to lay my head on Mommy! We got to cuddle, and she gave me lots of kisses.

Finally

The moment that played over and over in my dreams is finally a reality.
It's really happening, right in front of me!

Watching the nurses gently arrange all the tubes and cords and thangs.
Listening to the alarms rang and rang,
but this time, no worries or anxiety or heart pains.

Your tiny little body, wiggling and wiggling.
I'm smiling real big, showing all my fillings.
Waiting patiently, anxiously, subconsciously
panicking but ready to have you placed up against my heartbeat.

Kangaroo time, just you and me. Soft music faded in the background,
snuggled up in the hospital gown. Stiff as a board, having to pee,
but I don't care because it's just you and me!

The time on the clock seemed to be moving fast,
I just held you tighter, and at you, I stared.
After 49 days of craving, the day has finally appeared.
My tiny, little hero, you are so brave!
And I truly think it's my life you saved.

Thank you, son.
Mommy Loves you!

After four long months, Asher became stronger! Finally, after maintaining a healthy body temperature, the doctors determined that he could move from the incubator to a big boy crib.

A crib will be so cool! I'll get to see what everyone is doing throughout the day. I can see when Mommy is walking in. I can see my favorite doctors and nurses. I'm so close to going home now that I can feel it in my bones! This is awesome!

I am so happy. I can't wait until Mommy sees me in my big boy crib. I know she will be so happy. Storytime will be even better when Mommy sits with me. Once they take this tube out, she can pick me up and play with me whenever she wants.

The holiday season was approaching. Asher had been making good progress with his health and was on low-flow oxygen, which was good enough to go home. However, Asher wasn't growing enough for the doctors. Although Mommy knew the doctors were just being cautious due to his history, she was still sad and frustrated as she realized she wouldn't have him home for Thanksgiving.

Finally, after five months and six days, I get to go home! That is 159 days! Twenty-three weeks! How many hours? 3,816! That's 228,960 minutes! What is that in seconds? 13,737,600! Finally, I am busting out of the NICU! I am graduating!

I am so happy to be going home! I'm so glad to see the world outside of these hospital walls. I'm ready to feel the breeze, see the trees, and embrace the sun.

My entrance into this world was very abrupt. Yet, I fought my way past the ten percent chance of survival, beating the odds and making a stand. I'm truly grateful for all the support. I don't know how Mommy would have made it if your guys didn't show up. So, after five long months of fighting this fight, I get to go home to sleep with my family tonight.

Love Always,
The Tiny Hero, Asher Avery.

About Author

Tameka L. Tate, a Baton Rouge native, has always enjoyed writing, but the birth and loss of daughter Ayrii Ali pushed Tameka to write through the pain and inspired a renewed commitment to literature as a path to healing. The story of Asher is the harrowing and miraculous tale of Tameka's rainbow baby, born at just 23 weeks gestation and surviving for five months and six days in the NICU before finally coming home.

"I hope that anyone who reads this book will understand that with the smallest amount of faith and strength, anything is possible. To all the NICU moms, you are not alone. Fight for your tiny HERO and give yourself the grace to feel all of your feelings; because your voice and your feelings are valid." - Tameka Tate

www.ingramcontent.com/pod-product-compliance
Lightning Source LLC
Chambersburg PA
CBHW040726060526
44119CB00084B/341